EXCITING OUTDOOR CAREERS

ADVENTURE GUIDE

DWAYNE HICKS

PowerKiDS press

Published in 2026 by The Rosen Publishing Group, Inc.
2544 Clinton Street, Buffalo, NY 14224

First Edition

Editor: Greg Roza
Book Design: Rachel Rising

Photo Credits: Cover, p. 12 PeopleImages.com - Yuri A/Shutterstock.com; Cover, pp. 1, 3–24 Iurii Vlasenko/Shutterstock.com; Cover, pp. 1, 3–24 klyaksun/Shutterstock.com; p. 4 Blue Titan/Shutterstock.com; p. 5 Alex Brylov/Shutterstock.com; p. 6 vvoe/Shutterstock.com; p. 7 Dziewul/Shutterstock.com; p. 9 Alex Brylov/Shutterstock.com; p. 10 Ewan Chesser/Shutterstock.com; p. 11 FG Trade/iStock.com; p. 13 jack-sooksan/Shutterstock.com; p. 14 GoodFocused/Shutterstock.com; p. 15 miodrag ignjatovic/iStock.com; p. 17 Bob Pool/Shutterstock.com; p. 18 D and S Photography Archives/Alamy Stock Photo; p. 19 Featureflash Photo Agency/Shutterstock.com; p. 20 Lopolo/Shutterstock.com; p. 21 Smart-foto/Shutterstock.com.

Some of the images in this book illustrate individuals who are models. The depictions do not imply actual situations or events.

Cataloging-in-Publication Data

Names: Hicks, Dwayne.
Title: Adventure guide / Dwayne Hicks.
Description: Buffalo, New York : PowerKids Press, 2026. | Series: Exciting outdoor careers | Includes glossary and index.
Identifiers: ISBN 9781499457155 (pbk.) | ISBN 9781499457162 (library bound) | ISBN 9781499457179 (ebook)
Subjects: LCSH: Recreation leaders–Juvenile literature. | Tour guides (Persons)–Juvenile literature. | Adventure and adventurers–Vocational guidance–Juvenile literature. | Tourism–Vocational guidance–Juvenile literature. | Outdoor recreation–Vocational guidance–Juvenile literature.
Classification: LCC GV181.4 H54 2026 | DDC 790.02373–dc23

Manufactured in China

CPSIA Compliance Information: Batch #QWPK26. For Further Information contact Rosen Publishing at 1-800-237-9932.

CONTENTS

READY FOR ADVENTURE!

Do you consider yourself the "outdoorsy" type? Do you like hiking, camping, rafting, and similar activities? Imagine making a living doing those things. That's exactly what an adventure guide does!

Adventure guides aren't just campers and hikers—they're specialists. They're very knowledgeable about topics such hiking or camping or fishing. Some are **expert** skiers. Some are expert rafters. Some enjoy zip-lining and rock climbing. However, there's more to it than just enjoying outdoor activities. Adventure guides must be well trained in safety and first-aid. They must be good leaders with good **communication** skills. They have a solid understanding of local wildlife and landforms.

A successful adventure guide is someone who adventurers are happy to follow!

PREPARING TO GUIDE

The typical day for an adventure guide depends on the weather, location, and type of adventure. They must dress properly—this could be snowshoes and a parka, diving gear, or tall boots called hip waders for flyfishing.

An adventure guide's workday could be a typical 9-to-5 job, or it could be a camping trip that lasts several days. Adventure guides may need several hours or a day to prepare for a trip, which they get paid for as part of their duties. This could mean preparing lunches for hikers, packing **parachutes** for a skydiving trip, or repairing mosquito netting.

OUTDOOR ADVICE

An adventure guide may guide more than one group in a single day. They might take a group on a two-hour rafting tour at 10 a.m., and then guide another group at 2 p.m. In between, the guide prepares and repairs gear for the next group.

White water rafting guides must make sure the raft and other gear is ready to go before every adventure.

STRENGTH AND STAMINA

If you want to become an adventure guide, being physically fit is a good starting point. You need to be strong to hike for miles through a national park or to snowshoe several miles to reach a mountain cabin. Strength training will build your muscles.

In order to lead a group of adventurers, guides must have stamina. This means being strong enough to withstand a long period of exercise or **stress**. Stamina helps when leading a group of rock climbers up a cliff face. A great way to build stamina is to get outside and get moving—hiking, swimming, climbing, running, or whatever you like most.

OUTDOOR ADVICE

Hiking might be a great place to start when building your stamina. But other activities—organized sports, marital arts, swimming, and so on—will help make you a more well-rounded guide.

Rock climbing guides need to take a month-long training course before they can start leading adventurers up mountains.

TALENTS AND KNOWLEDGE

Some people have natural talents or skills they learned when they were younger, whether it's riding a horse, setting up a camp, or scuba diving. These talents can help you land a job as a guide. However, there's plenty more you need to learn.

Guides must understand the **environment** in which they work. A hiking guide needs to know the trails and **terrain** of the location. White water rafting guides need to understand the danger surrounding rapids and waterfalls. Guides need to have a complete understanding of the tools and gear related to the tour. They need to know which plants and animals are dangerous.

OUTDOOR ADVICE

Adventure guides need to be trained in first aid, **CPR**, and survival skills. Sometimes employers will insist on and provide the training for these.

Some adventure guides have a college degree. This could be in environmental **conservation**, zoology, or park management, among others.

FOLLOW ME!

Adventure guides need to be good leaders. This is what they were hired for—to lead! Good leadership skills include listening to others and communicating instructions clearly. Guides know how to respond to arguments and disagreements within the group, which helps keep everyone happy and on time. Guides must be able to respond to **emergencies** calmly and efficiently.

Regardless of what happens, guides must remain calm and in charge. If a hiker fell and broke their leg, for example, the guide is expected to know how to respond. If the guide panics, just think how that will affect the rest of the group.

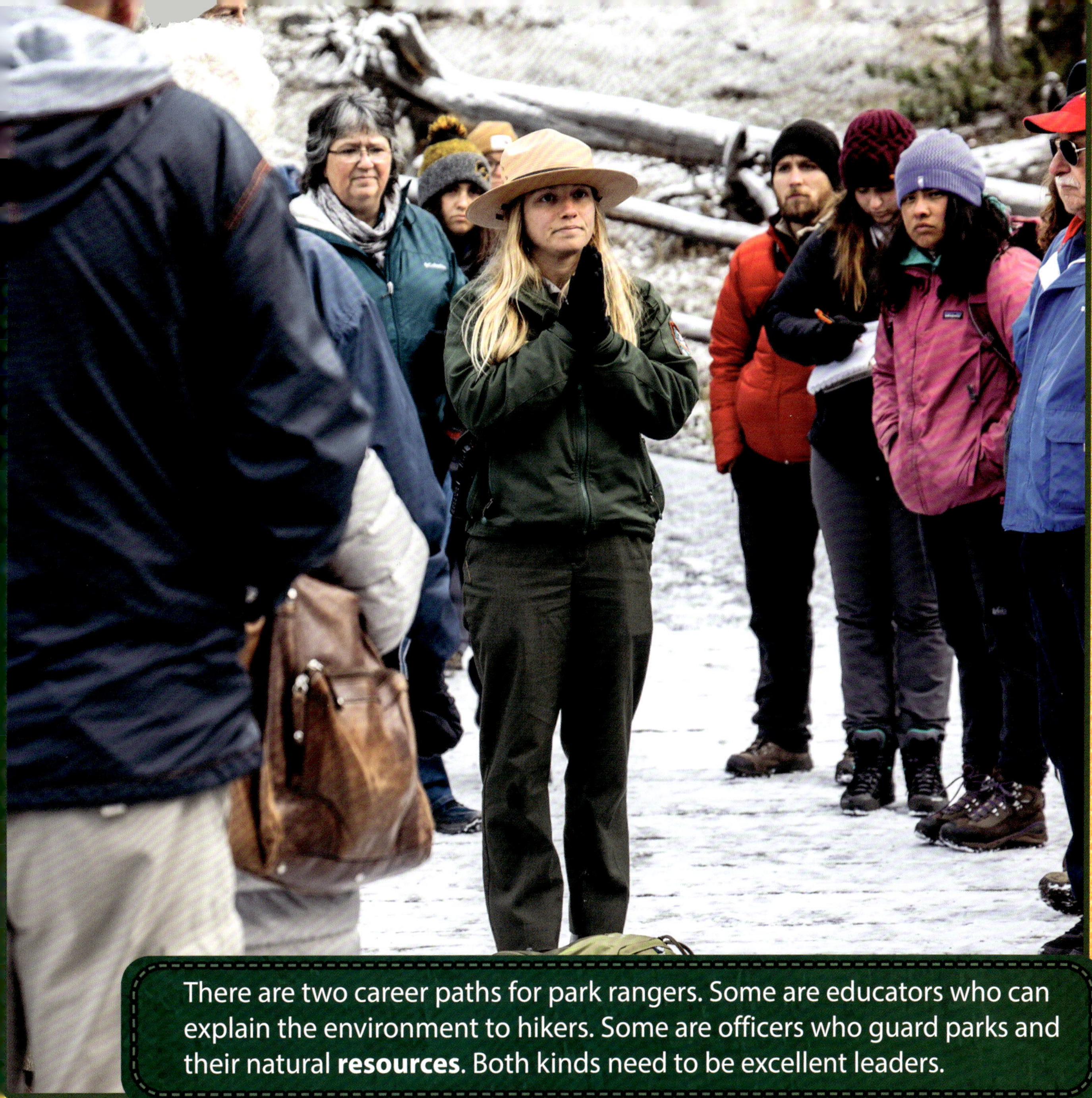

There are two career paths for park rangers. Some are educators who can explain the environment to hikers. Some are officers who guard parks and their natural **resources**. Both kinds need to be excellent leaders.

TIME TO TEACH

Adventure guides are teachers. Part of the joy of going on an adventure tour is learning as much as you can about the activity, the environment, and survival skills. Guides teach adventurers facts about the location such as the wildlife, terrain, weather, and landforms. A fishing guide will know all about the safety of the location, the kinds of fish there, how to collect and use bait, and more. Rock climbing guides will know which areas are too difficult for the group, and which paths will make the experience enjoyable. A **snorkeling** guide will tell you which fish are safe and which are dangerous.

Most adventure guides have a knack for teaching others what they know. It can be one of the most fulfilling parts of the job.

KEEP THEM ENTERTAINED

Adventure guides are usually outgoing people. They are usually good entertainers. Simply smiling and joking around with adventurers helps put everyone at ease in potentially dangerous surroundings. Oftentimes, guides have a set script for each tour, which could include jokes and humorous stories. Adventure guides are good at using their training and talents to wow adventurers and encourage them to join in the excitement.

Some adventure guides work for wildlife farms and **sanctuaries**. They lead educational shows for visitors. These shows often include entertaining, daring, or humorous moments, often between the speaker and the animals they are discussing.

OUTDOOR ADVICE

Many adventure guides receive tips from adventurers. The more entertained an adventurer feels, the more they are likely to tip their guides.

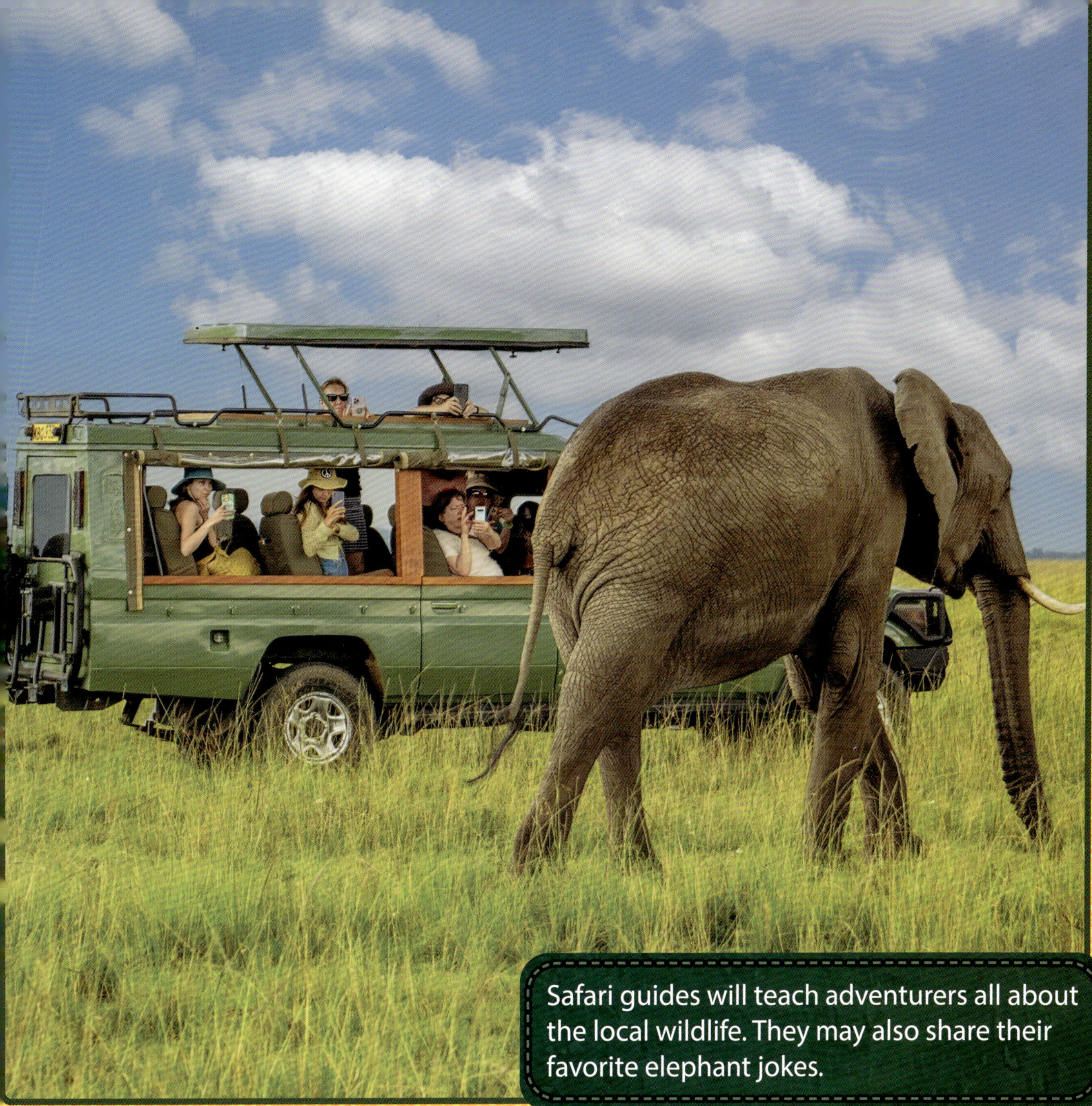

Safari guides will teach adventurers all about the local wildlife. They may also share their favorite elephant jokes.

FAMOUS ADVENTURE GUIDES

Nepalese Tibetan mountain climber Tenzing Norgay was a **Sherpa** who famously led New Zealander Edmund Hillary to the top of Mount Everest in 1953. The duo became the first people to accomplish such a feat! In 1954, the Indian government created the Field Training Himalayan Institute and made Norgay the first director.

Sadly, Irwin died doing what he loved. He was killed by a stingray while filming a segment for a show titled *Ocean's Deadliest*.

Steve Irwin was a zoologist and environmentalist from Australia. He is remembered as "The Crocodile Hunter," which was the name of his television show. Through his show, Irwin led millions of people on guided tours of some of Australia's wildest environments. Irwin's wife and children are also environmentalists.

THE SKY'S THE LIMIT!

Can one make a living as an adventure guide? It depends on the job and how long it lasts. Some jobs are seasonal, which means you won't make money all year round. Adventure guide pay ranges from $50 a day to more than $500 a day.

If this sounds like a good career fit for you, you can start preparing right now for an adventure guide job. Staying physically fit and learning all you can about outdoor activities is a great start. Other areas of study may include animal management, plant identification, first aid, and forestry, to name a few.

OUTDOOR ADVICE

Some guided adventure tours are easy, such as a walk through a state park. Others, such as skydiving, are far more extreme! You can follow the path you most enjoy.

The sky is the limit—literally—when seeking a career as an adventure guide!

GLOSSARY

communication: The use of words, sounds, signs, or behaviors to convey ideas, thoughts, and feelings.

conservation: Efforts to care for the natural world.

CPR: A procedure used to restore normal breathing when the heart stops beating. Short for cardiopulmonary resuscitation.

emergency: An unexpected situation that calls for immediate action.

environment: The conditions that surround a living thing and affect the way it lives.

expert: Someone who knows a great deal about something.

parachute: Something shaped like an umbrella used to slow down a person who is falling through the air.

resource: Something that can be used.

sanctuary: An area of land set aside to allow animals to live without being bothered or hunted by people.

Sherpa: A member of a group of people living on the high southern slopes of the Himalayas who are known for providing support for hikers and mountain climbers.

snorkel: To swim underwater with a curved tube that extends above the surface of the water for breathing.

stress: Something that causes strong feelings of worry.

terrain: A type of land in an area.

FOR MORE INFORMATION

BOOKS

Allan, John. *The Outdoor Survival Guide for Kids*. London, UK: Beetle Books, 2025.

Furneaux, Ky. *Adventure Awaits: The Beginner's Guide to the Great Outdoors*. London, UK: Applesauce Press, 2025.

WEBSITES

Steve Irwin – The Crocodile Hunter & Wildlife Warrior
aussieanimals.com/notable-figures/steve-irwin
This detailed website has a lot more information about Crocodile Hunter Steve Irwin.

Tenzing Norgay Facts for Kids
kids.kiddle.co/Tenzing_Norgay
Read all about the life of famous adventure guide Tenzing Norgay.

Publisher's note to educators and parents: Our editors have carefully reviewed these websites to ensure that they are suitable for students. Many websites change frequently, however, and we cannot guarantee that a site's future contents will continue to meet our high standards of quality and educational value. Be advised that students should be closely supervised whenever they access the internet.

INDEX